Alyssa Barlow

Scott Anthony Barlow

Family Passport

Kids Travel Journal

A Family Adventure to Remember

Copyright © Family Passport, 2018

ISBN-13: 978-1987650853
ISBN-10: 1987650859

Illustrations from Freepik

Thank You Letter

Dear _____

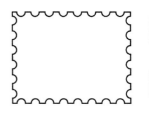

Thank you for letting us stay in your home.

We were have stayed for _____ days. My favorite thing

about it was _____

I took care of your home by _____

Thank you for sharing your home!

From,

_____

About the Authors

(and possibly more important, the authors' kids)

Scott and Alyssa Barlow have three adventurous kids that tend to climb trees in parks where it may or may not be ok with the people who run the park. Their names are Mackenzie, Camden and Grayson and they love exploring, are so curious that they can ask "why" 47 times in three minutes and they learned after going to Europe that they absolutely love crepes (especially with chocolate and bananas)

Alyssa Barlow (aside from being a mother) taught Kindergarten and First Grade for 10 years and has been surrounded by education in her family her whole life. She is also a fitness instructor, baker of a mean black bean brownie and lover of chocolate croissants.

Scott Barlow has been in online publishing, training & instructional design and Human Resources for the last 15 years. He also is the CEO of Happen to Your Career which helps people find and do work they love!

Both Scott and Alyssa love to travel and share much of what they've learned at http://familypassport.co/podcast

Made in the USA
Las Vegas, NV
07 January 2022

40736328R00052

Where will your passport take you?

How will you remember?

We are so excited
for you and your children to share
and record your amazing adventure!!!

No matter where your journey begins and ends you can help your child record their favorite memories and experiences. As well as some great real world application skills and projects!!!

This journal is written in an easy to follow fill in the blank format with lots of room for your child to write and draw about their daily adventures.

Created based on the Barlow Family's experiences traveling in Portugal and Paris. For more about their adventures visit familypassport.co

For ages 5-8

ISBN 9781987650853

900

9 781987 650853

Restaurant Review

Restaurant Overall

Date: ....

Restaurant Name

....

Server name

....

Would you recommend this restaurant to another family?

....

Clean

_____

Something to do at table

_____

Wait time to sit

_____

Service

Friendly

_____

Helped pick food/read menu

_____

Time to order

_____

Food

Taste

_____

Temp

_____

Time to receive

_____

Your Adventure Plan

Kids Day Out in ....

Ideas

-
-
-
-
-
-
-

Budget ....   Days available ....

Top Pick!

Cost: _____   Travel needed: _____

Activities I want to do: _____

_____

wwwwwwwwwwwwwwwwwwwwwwwwwwwwwwwwwwwwwwwwwwww

Second Pick!

Cost: _____   Travel needed: _____

Activities I want to do: _____

_____

Alphabet Pages:

Have your child write or draw what they see that begins with the corresponding letter of the alphabet. Example Nortre Dame would go in the space for letter N.

Y

Z

Alphabet Pages:

Have your child write or draw what they see that begins with the corresponding letter of the alphabet. Example Nortre Dame would go in the space for letter N.

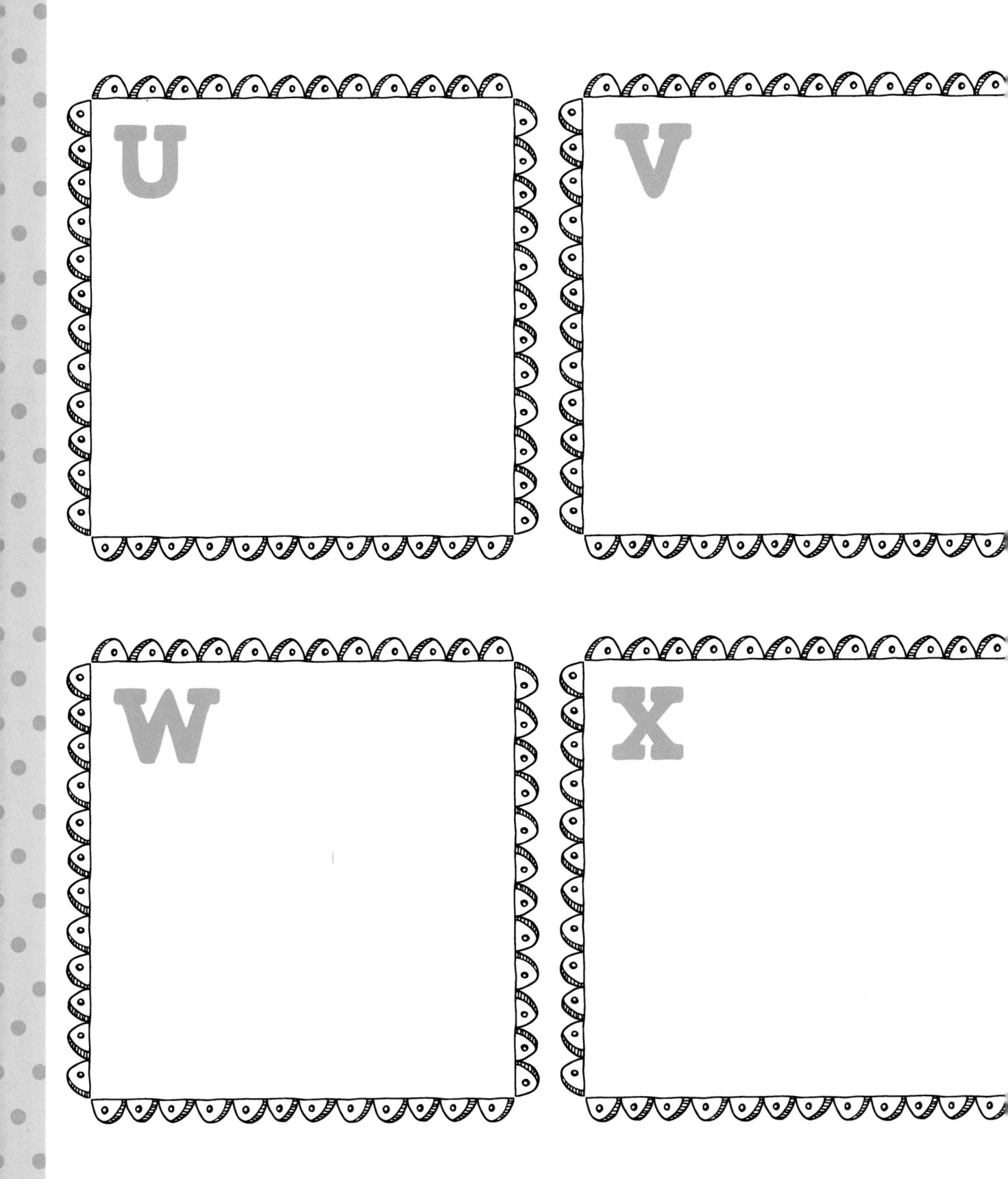

Alphabet Pages:

Have your child write or draw what they see that begins with the corresponding letter of the alphabet. Example Nortre Dame would go in the space for letter N.

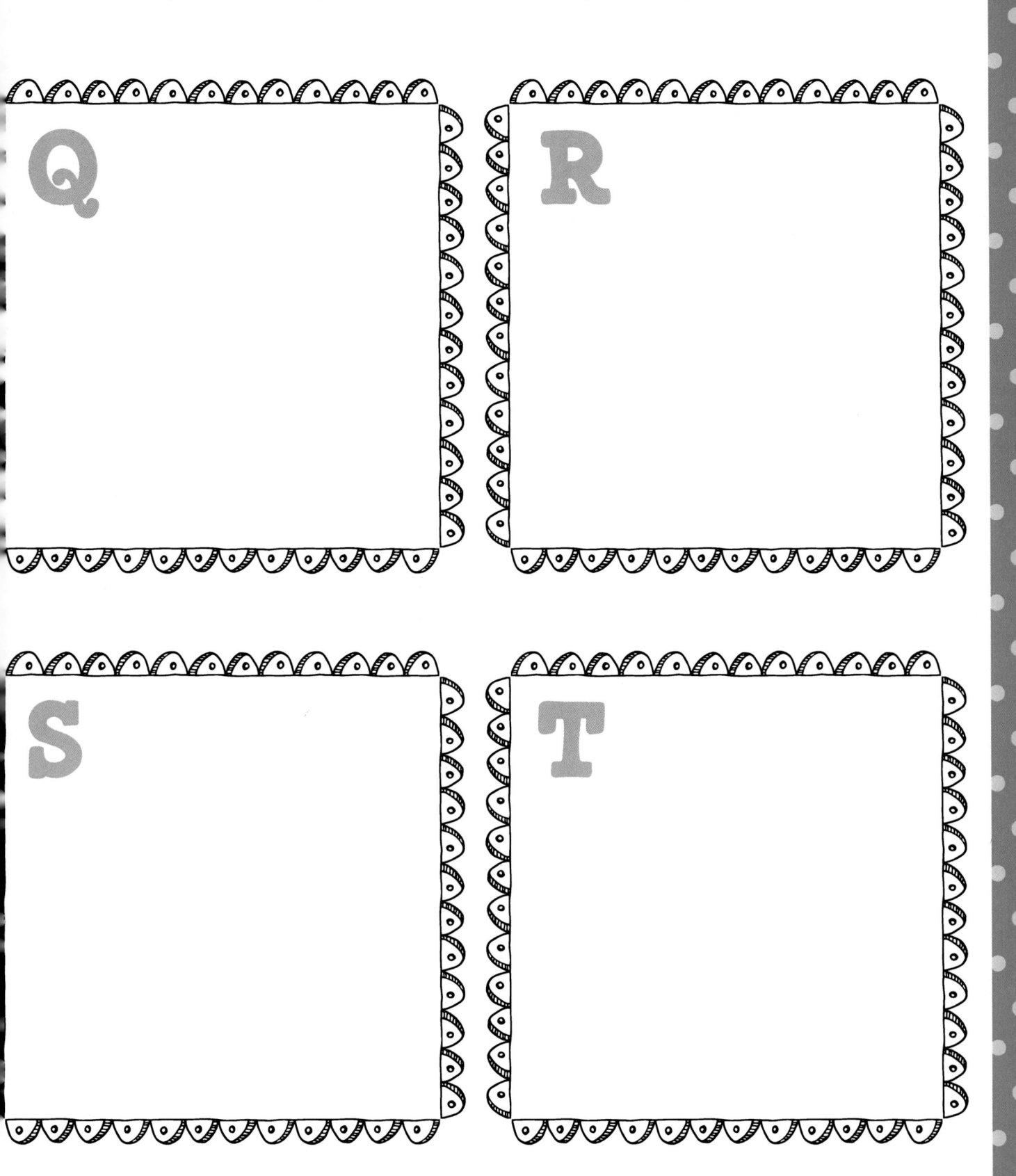

Q

R

S

T

Alphabet Pages:

Have your child write or draw what they see that begins with the corresponding letter of the alphabet. Example Nortre Dame would go in the space for letter N.

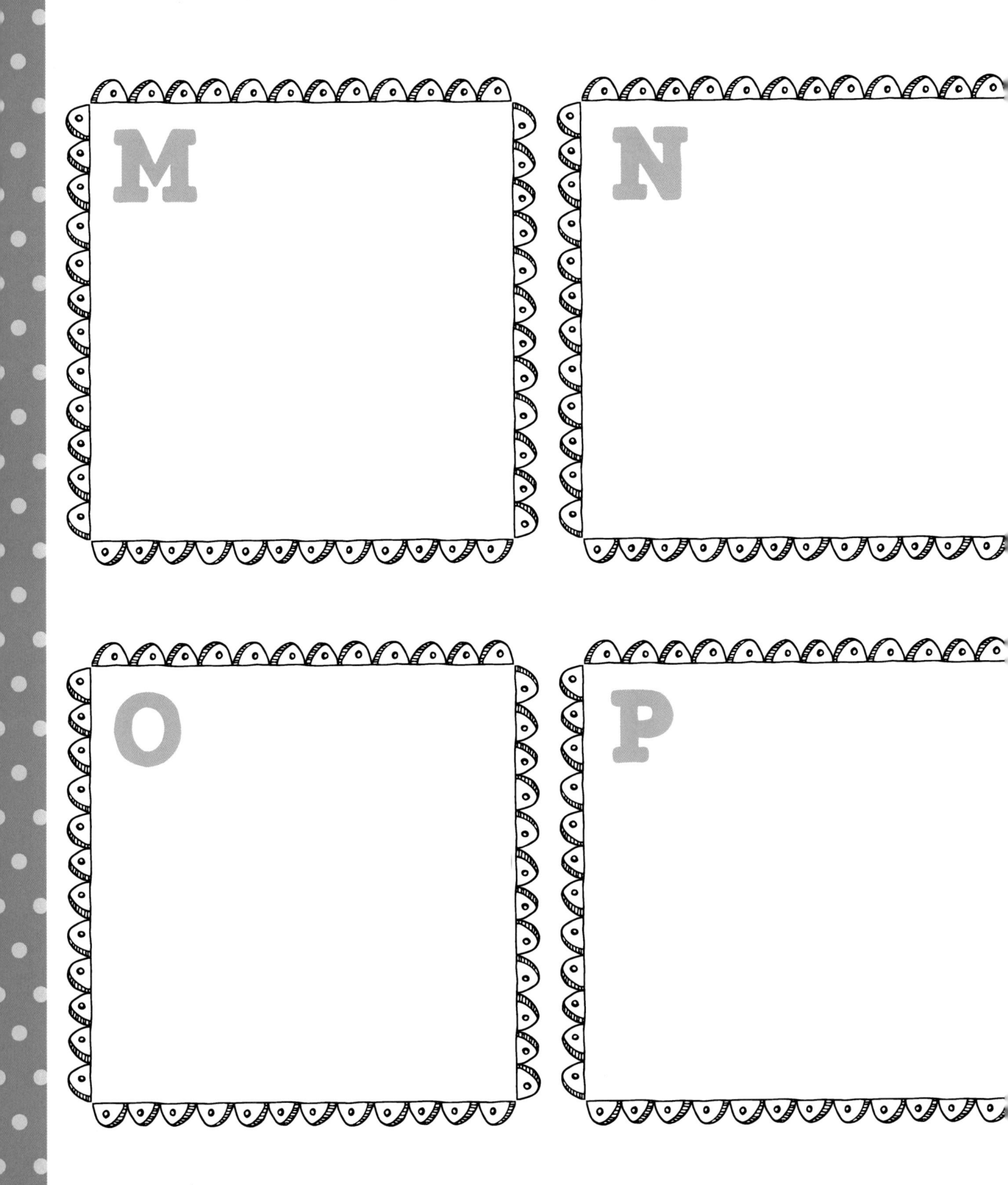

M

N

O

P

Alphabet Pages:

Have your child write or draw what they see that begins with the corresponding letter of the alphabet. Example Nortre Dame would go in the space for letter N.

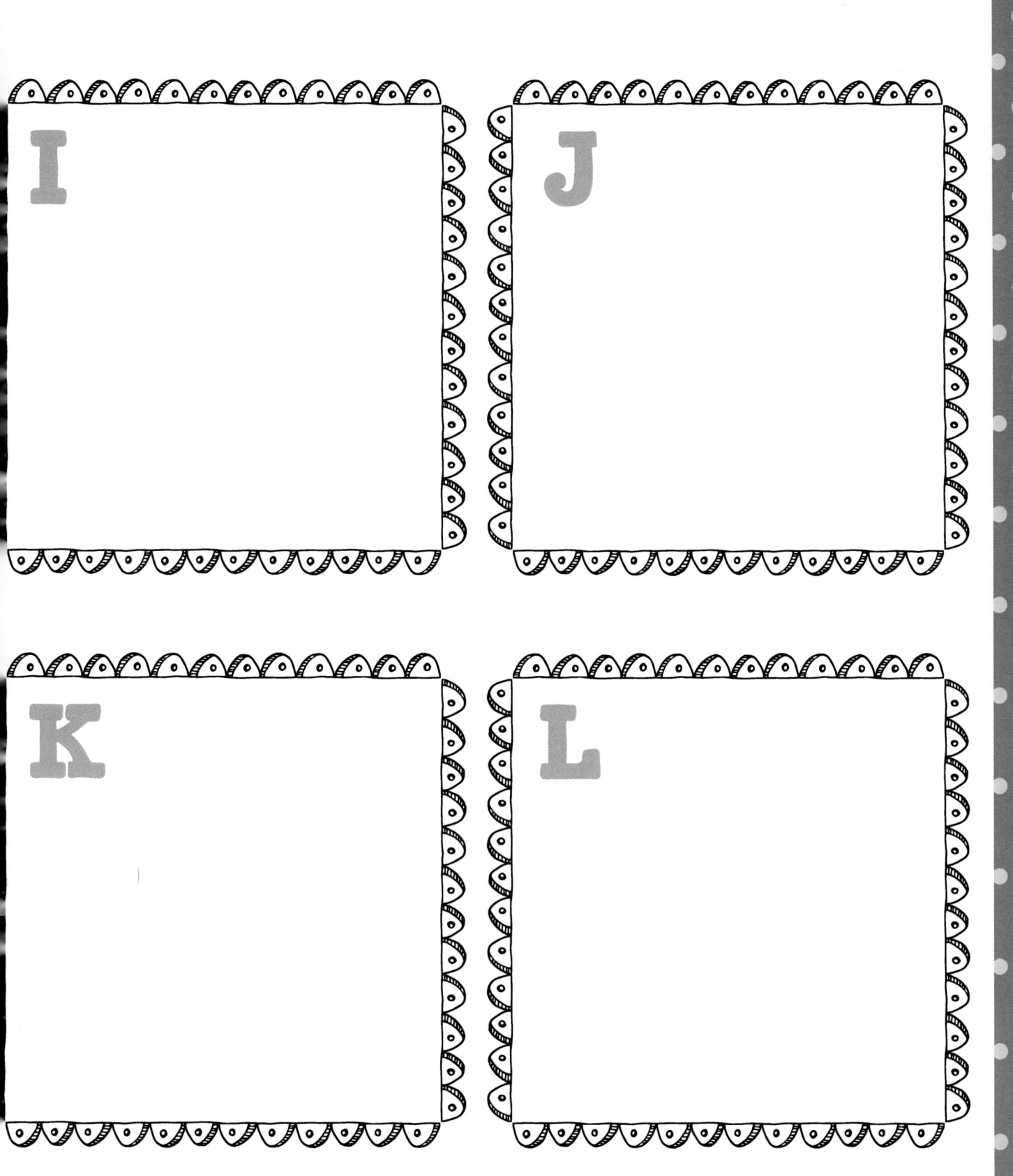

Alphabet Pages:

Have your child write or draw what they see that begins with the corresponding letter of the alphabet. Example Nortre Dame would go in the space for letter N.

Bonus Activities

Write or Draw Alphabet

Have your child write or draw what they see that begins with the corresponding letter of the alphabet. Example Nortre Dame would go in the space for letter N.

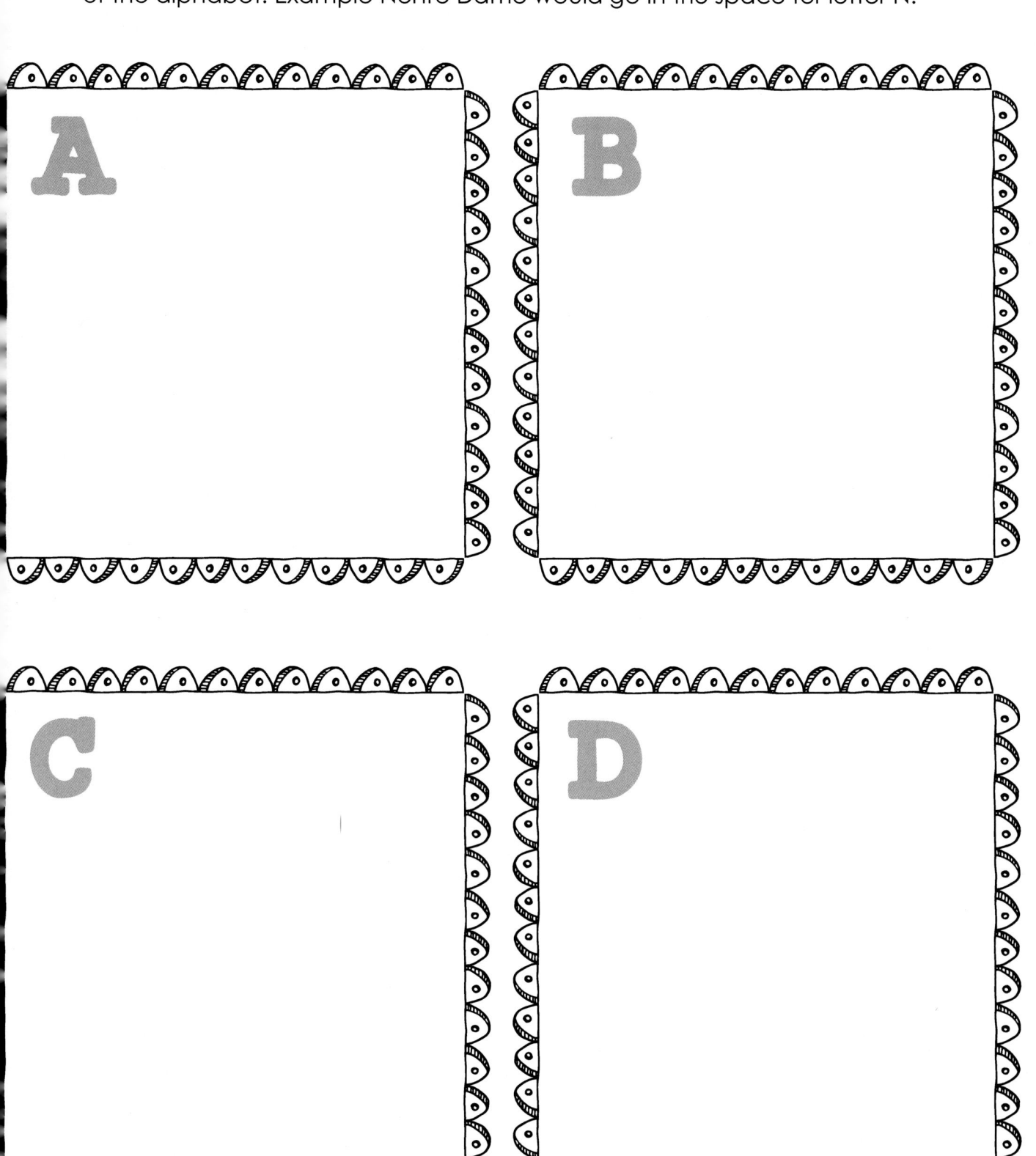

Souvenirs

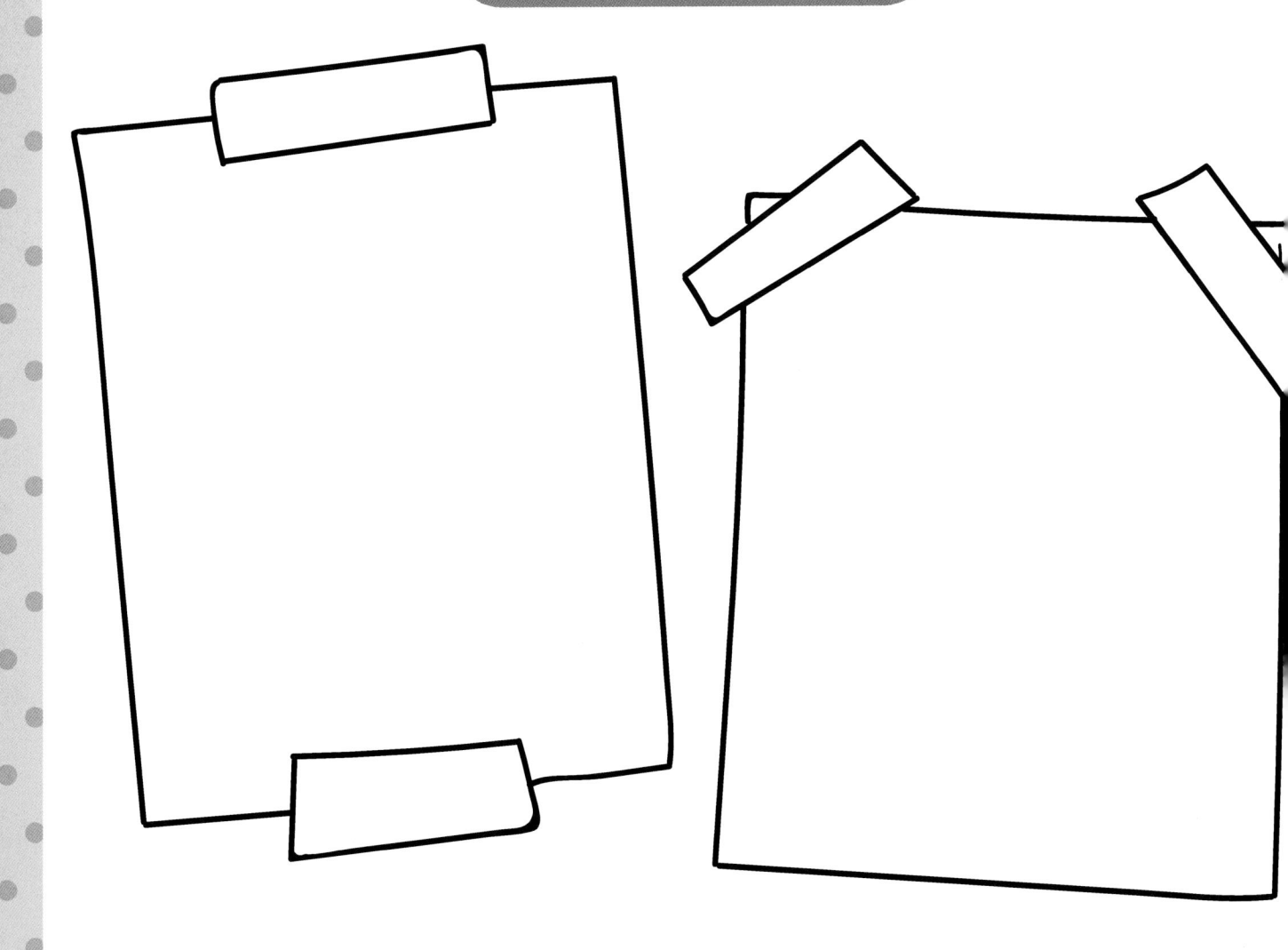

Paste or tape mementos from your adventure here

The best day was

My favorite food was

_____

_____

_____

_____

My favorite thing that we did was

_____

_____

_____

Last Day!

Today I am excited to go home to see

_____

_____

_____

_____

The thing I will miss the most about our trip

_____

_____

_____

My favorite part about our trip was

_____

_____

_____

Today

I was most excited to see

_____
_____
_____
_____
_____
_____

I want to

Remember

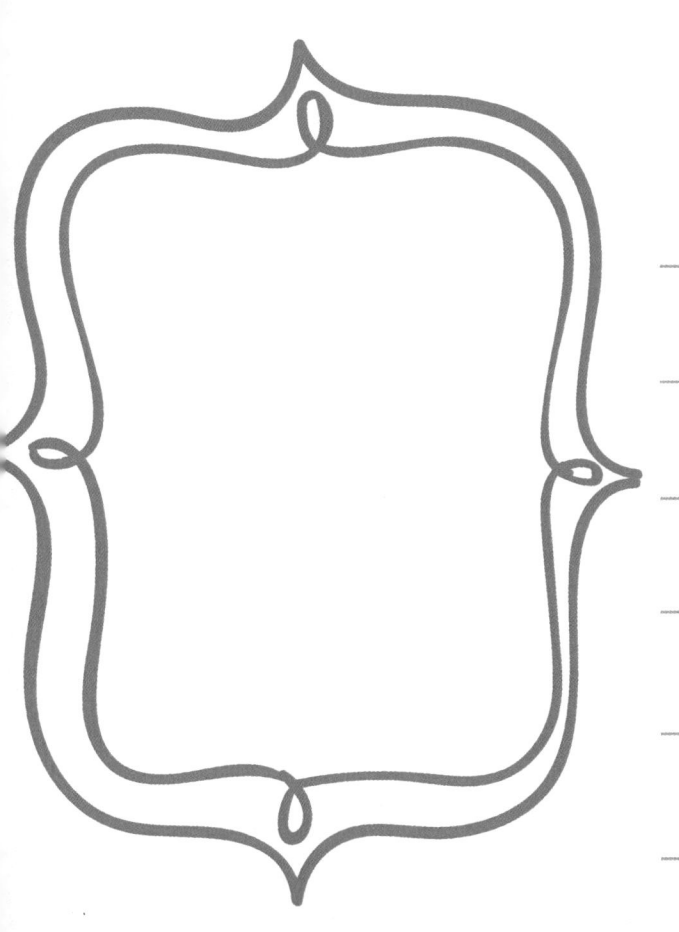

_____
_____
_____
_____
_____

Daily Journal

day #

Location: ....

Today

The weather was _____

and the temperature was

_____

My favorite food
we tried today was

Today we traveled by

....

Today we went to see

_____

_____

_____

_____

Remember

I want to

I was most excited to see

Today

Daily Journal

day #

Location: ....

Today

The weather was

_____

and the temperature was

_____

My favorite food we tried today was

Today we went to see ....

_____

_____

_____

_____

_____

Today we traveled by ....

_____
_____
_____
_____

Remember

I want to

_____
_____
_____
_____

I was most excited to see

Today

Daily Journal

day #

Location: ....

Today

The weather was

_____

and the temperature was

_____

My favorite food
we tried today was

Today we went to see

_____

_____

_____

_____

_____

_____

Today we traveled by

....

Today

I was most excited to see

_____

_____

_____

_____

_____

_____

I want to

Remember

_____

_____

_____

_____

_____

_____

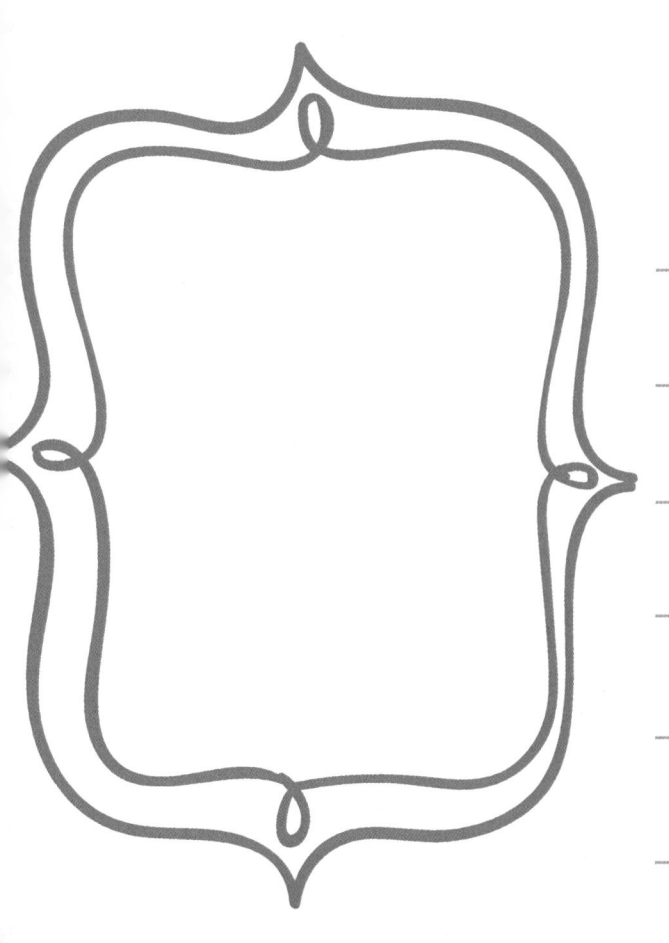

Daily Journal

day #

Location: ....

Today

The weather was _____

and the temperature was

My favorite food
we tried today was

_____

Today we traveled by

....

Today we went to see

_____

_____

_____

_____

Remember

I want to

I was most excited to see

Today

Daily Journal

day #

Location: ....

 **Today**

The weather was

_____

and the temperature was

_____

Today we went to see   ....

_____

_____

_____

_____

_____

My favorite food we tried today was

Today we traveled by   ....

Remember

I want to

I was most excited to see

Today

Daily Journal

day #

Location: ....

Today

The weather was

_____

and the temperature was

_____

My favorite food
we tried today was

Today we went to see

_____

_____

_____

_____

_____

_____

Today we traveled by

....

Today

I was most excited to see

_____

_____

_____

_____

_____

_____

I want to

Remember

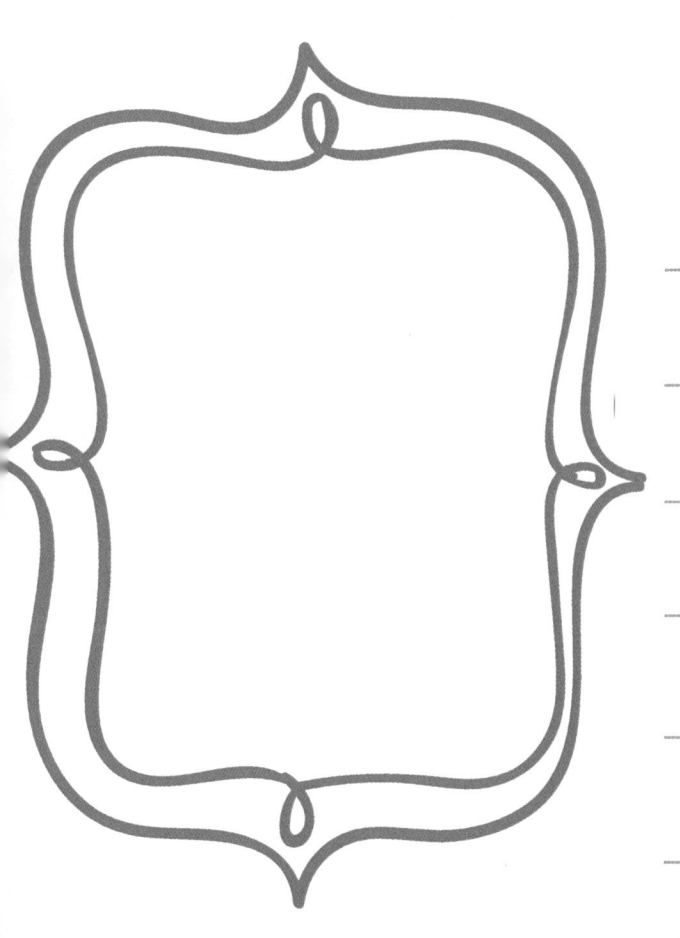

_____

_____

_____

_____

_____

Daily Journal

day #

Location: ....

Today

The weather was _____

and the temperature was

_____

My favorite food
we tried today was

Today we traveled by

....

Today we went to see

_____

_____

_____

_____

Remember

I want to

Today

I was most excited to see

Daily Journal

day #

Location: ....

The weather was

_____

and the temperature was

_____

My favorite food we tried today was

Today we went to see ....

_____

_____

_____

_____

_____

Today we traveled by ....

Today

I was most excited to see

_____

_____

_____

_____

_____

Remember

I want to

_____

_____

_____

_____

_____

Daily Journal

day #

Location: ....

Today

The weather was

_____

and the temperature was

_____

My favorite food
we tried today was

Today we went to see

_____

_____

_____

_____

_____

_____

Today we traveled by

....

Remember

I want to

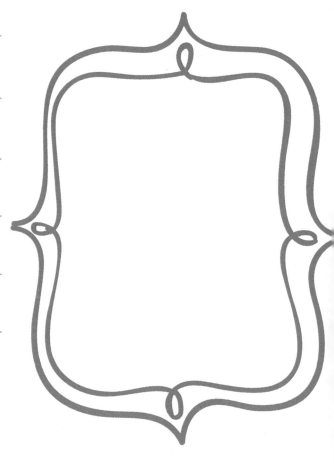

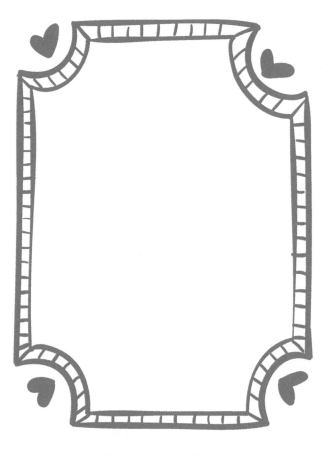

I was most excited to see

Today

Daily Journal

day #

Location: ....

The weather was _____

and the temperature was

My favorite food
we tried today was

_____

Today we traveled by

....

Today we went to see

_____

_____

_____

_____

Remember

I want to

_____

Today

I was most excited to see

Daily Journal

day #

Location: ....

Today

The weather was

_____

and the temperature was

_____

My favorite food we tried today was

Today we went to see ....

_____

_____

_____

_____

_____

Today we traveled by ....

Today

I was most excited to see

_____
_____
_____
_____
_____

Remember

I want to

_____
_____
_____
_____
_____

Daily Journal

day #

Location: ....

Today

The weather was

_____

and the temperature was

_____

My favorite food
we tried today was

Today we went to see

_____

_____

_____

_____

_____

_____

Today we traveled by

....

Today

I was most excited to see

_____

_____

_____

_____

_____

_____

I want to

Remember

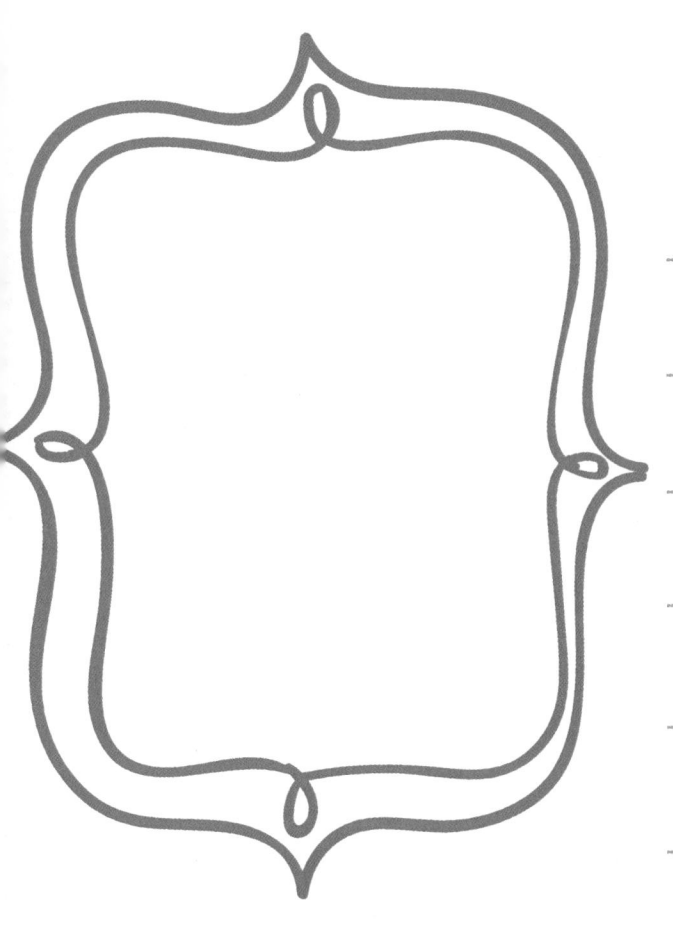

_____

_____

_____

_____

_____

_____

Hello and Thank You
for choosing the
Family Passport Kids Travel Journal!

We are excited to share with you one of the many ways we found to help our kids make the most out of our family adventures!!! Our goal is for your family to make the most of your travels and everlasting memories to share!!!

When we created this for our 3 children, we wanted to keep their brains working while we traveled, as well as allow them to record what was meaningful to them on the trip. We found journaling to be a great way to keep them reading and writing while away from school, and recording their favorite memories.

Best of all, it helped us learn many amazing things about our children and grow closer to them during this experience. We also learned that what we thought was cool, was way different than our kids. We would be enamored by the beautiful buildings and our kids would come home and write about the pigeons or the subway ride!!! This was also a great way for us to learn about our kids learning styles and to help foster the learning process even after we had our amazing adventure.

We looked for a journal before the trip but nothing stood out to us. We learned so much just having them write on paper. Our oldest even transferred her writing to a blog so her class back home could follow along. The younger two brought their journals to school when we returned home.

After having such a positive experience, we wanted to create something for other traveling families to use that was an easy format to capture all that you want to remember, even if it was the pigeons on their head!!! And for us to use on our future trips too!!

We'd love to hear what you and your kids think or any ideas you had to make journaling a fun experience for your family!

Drop us an email anytime at Alyssa@familypassport.co

Alyssa and Scott

What's in this Journal Anyway?

Before My Trip:

Record all the information you have in preparation for the trip. There is even a page to brainstorm things you will need to pack. (Find our packing list at www.familypassport.co) Help your child write or have your child dictate the answers to the questions.

Journal Entry Pages:

Write where you are visiting and the number for each day of your trip. Then help them write the date and record the weather. Next, your child will answers questions about their day. These are great discussion points for you your child. Help your child write or draw their answers. The second entry page is for them to record their favorite memory of the day, remember those pigeons, this is where they would show up.

Last Day:

Record your favorite memories here. Two pages with space to record all your favorites!!!

Bonus Pages

Kids Day Out:

A planning page for your child to pick the events of one day of your trip. Give them a budget for the day, timeline and let them get creative. Our guidelines were it had to pay for the whole family, including travel and food if needed. We found this to be a great real world application. This was one of our kids favorite activities and of course days!!

Alphabet Pages:

Have your child write or draw what they see that begins with the corresponding letter of the alphabet. Example Nortre Dame would go in the space for letter N.

Restaurant review:

You can tear this page out and take it to a restaurant you eat at. It's a great way to get your kids thinking about all that goes on in a restaurant as well as keeping them entertained while waiting for food.

Thank you letter:

This page can be taken out and left for or mailed to the host if you stay at an Air B and B. We talked with our children how someone was letting us borrow their home, so we could have an amazing adventure. Some of you might even be lucky enough to meet your host!!

Supplies needed:

- Pencil

Optional Supplies:

- Crayons
- Markers
- Colored pencils
- Tape
- Envelope (to keep mementos in)

Hello,
Amazing Adventurer!

Now that your parents have read the instructions, you are ready to get started.

This page is all about you!!!

Now you can get started on your journal for the adventure that is coming. Start by filling in all your information. Then you will write all about your trip before you go and plan what to pack in your bags!! The rest is of course for your memories of each day of your trip!!! Don't forget to check out the bonus activities at the end of the journal. You can also find more bonus activities by asking your parents to go to www.familypassport.co/bonus

Your adventure awaits!!

Get started on recording your memories!!

My Adventure Passport

Name:_____

Age:_____   Grade:_____

Height:_____   Weight:_____

Draw or paste a photo
of yourself

Where the adventure begins:

_____

Before My Trip

I am going to

· ·

We are leaving on

· ·

I am excited about

_____

_____

_____

_____

_____

_____

_____

I am nervous about

_____

_____

_____

_____

_____

We will get there by

· ·

We will return home on

· ·

Packing List

Things I need everyday

_____

_____

_____

_____

_____

_____

Clothing needed

_____

_____

_____

_____

_____

Things I want to have to play with

_____

_____

_____

_____

Things I want to take from my room

_____

_____

_____

_____

Supplies I need for journal/school work

_____

_____

Daily Journal

day #

Location: ....

Today

The weather was

_____

and the temperature was

_____

My favorite food
we tried today was

Today we went to see

_____

_____

_____

_____

_____

_____

Today we traveled by
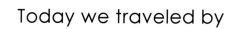

....

Today

I was most excited to see

_____
_____
_____
_____
_____

I want to

Remember

_____
_____
_____
_____
_____

Daily Journal

day #

Location: ....

Today

The weather was

_____

and the temperature was

_____

My favorite food we tried today was

Today we went to see ....

_____

_____

_____

_____

_____

Today we traveled by ....

Today

I was most excited to see

_____

_____

_____

_____

_____

_____

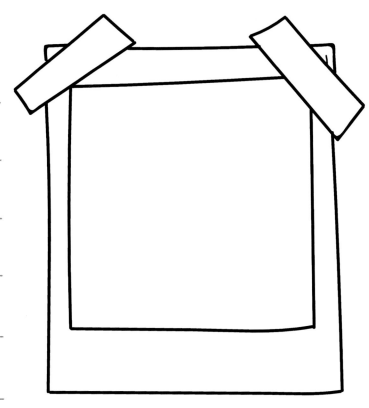

I want to

Remember

_____

_____

_____

_____

_____

_____

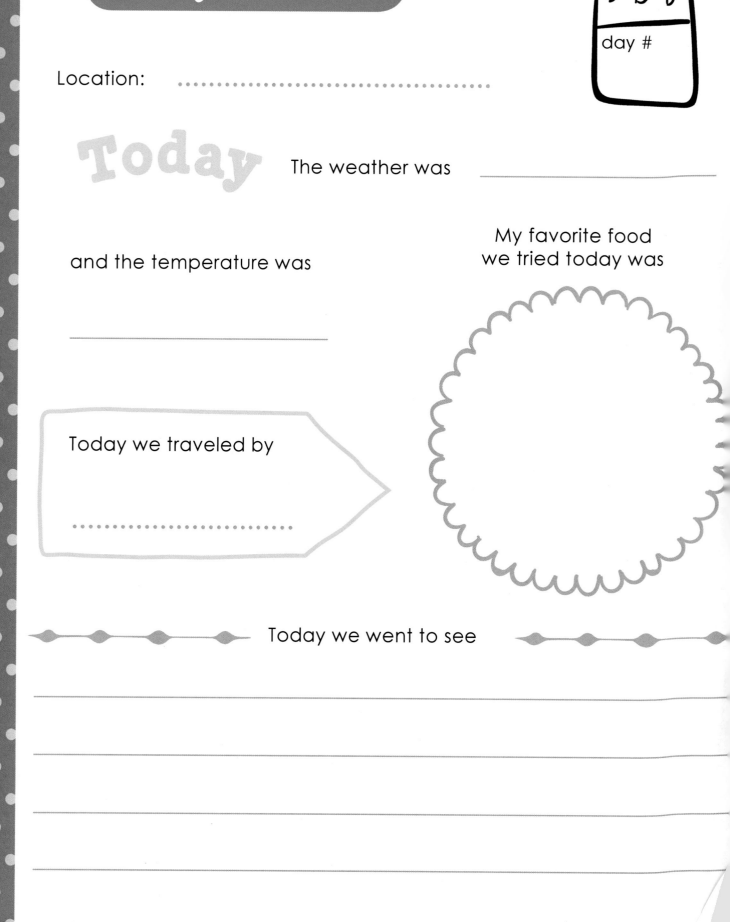

Daily Journal

day #

Location: ....

Today

The weather was _____

and the temperature was

My favorite food
we tried today was

_____

Today we traveled by

....

Today we went to see

_____

_____

_____

_____

Today

I was most excited to see

_____

_____

_____

_____

_____

_____

I want to

Remember

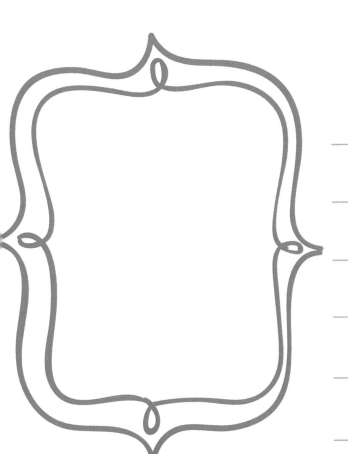

_____

_____

_____

_____

_____

Daily Journal

day #

Location: ....

Today

The weather was

_____

and the temperature was

_____

My favorite food
we tried today was

Today we went to see

_____

_____

_____

_____

_____

_____

Today we traveled by

....

Today

I was most excited to see

_____

_____

_____

_____

_____

I want to

Remember

_____

_____

_____

_____

_____

Daily Journal

day #

Location: ....

Today

The weather was

_____

and the temperature was

_____

My favorite food we tried today was

Today we went to see ....

_____

_____

_____

_____

_____

Today we traveled by ....

Today

I was most excited to see

_____
_____
_____
_____
_____
_____

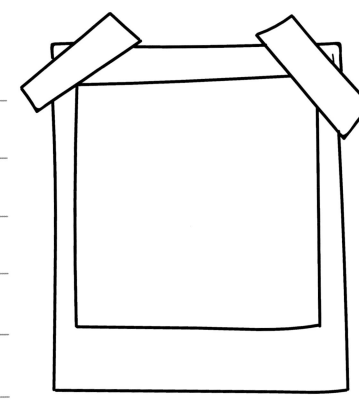

I want to

Remember

_____
_____
_____
_____

Daily Journal

day #

Location: ....

Today

The weather was _____

and the temperature was

_____

My favorite food
we tried today was

Today we traveled by

....

Today we went to see

_____

_____

_____

_____

Today

I was most excited to see

_____

_____

_____

_____

_____

_____

I want to

Remember

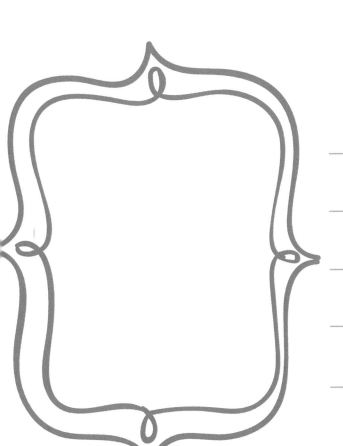

_____

_____

_____

_____

_____

Daily Journal

day #

Location: ....

Today

The weather was

_____

and the temperature was

_____

My favorite food
we tried today was

Today we went to see

_____
_____
_____
_____
_____
_____

Today we traveled by

....

Today

I was most excited to see

_____

_____

_____

_____

_____

I want to

Remember

_____

_____

_____

_____

_____

Daily Journal

day #

Location: ....

Today

The weather was

_____

and the temperature was

_____

My favorite food we tried today was

Today we went to see ....

_____

_____

_____

_____

_____

Today we traveled by ....

Today

I was most excited to see

_____

_____

_____

_____

_____

_____

I want to

Remember

_____

_____

_____

_____

_____

Daily Journal

day #

Location: ....

Today

The weather was
_____

and the temperature was

_____

My favorite food
we tried today was

Today we traveled by

....

Today we went to see

_____

_____

_____

_____

Today

I was most excited to see

_____

_____

_____

_____

_____

I want to

Remember

_____

_____

_____

_____

_____

_____

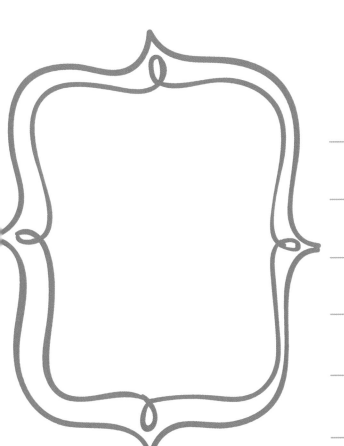

Daily Journal

day #

Location: ....

Today

The weather was

_____

and the temperature was

_____

My favorite food
we tried today was

Today we went to see

_____
_____
_____
_____
_____
_____

Today we traveled by

....

Today

I was most excited to see

_____
_____
_____
_____
_____

I want to

Remember

_____
_____
_____
_____

Daily Journal

day #

Location: ....

Today

The weather was

_____

and the temperature was

_____

My favorite food we tried today was

Today we went to see ....

_____

_____

_____

_____

_____

Today we traveled by ....

Today

I was most excited to see

_____
_____
_____
_____
_____
_____

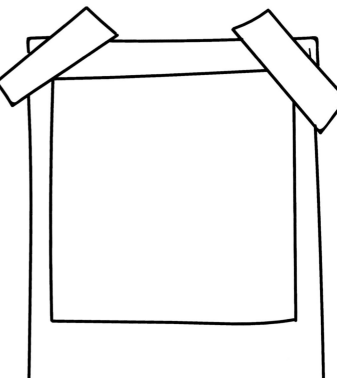

I want to

Remember

_____
_____
_____
_____
_____
_____

Daily Journal

day #

Location: ....

Today

The weather was _____

and the temperature was

My favorite food
we tried today was

_____

Today we traveled by

....

Today we went to see

_____

_____

_____

_____

_____

Today

I was most excited to see

_____
_____
_____
_____
_____
_____

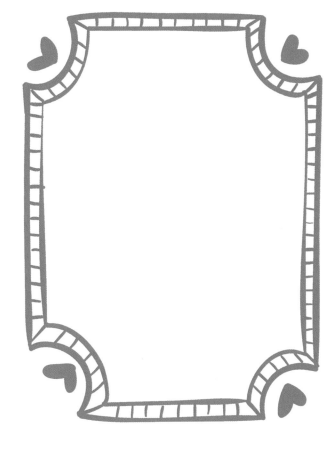

I want to

Remember

_____
_____
_____
_____
_____

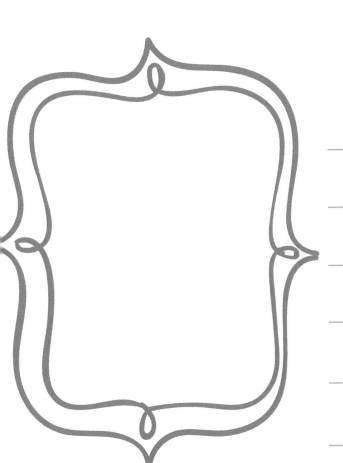

Daily Journal

day #

Location: ....

Today

The weather was

_____

and the temperature was

_____

My favorite food
we tried today was

Today we went to see

_____

_____

_____

_____

_____

_____

Today we traveled by

....

Today

I was most excited to see

_____
_____
_____
_____
_____
_____

I want to

Remember

_____
_____
_____
_____
_____
_____

Daily Journal

day #

Location: ....

Today

The weather was

_____

and the temperature was

_____

My favorite food we tried today was

Today we went to see ....

_____

_____

_____

_____

_____

Today we traveled by ....

Today

I was most excited to see

_____

_____

_____

_____

_____

_____

_____

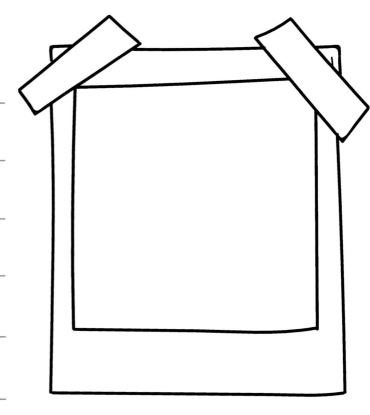

I want to

Remember

_____

_____

_____

_____

_____

Daily Journal

day #

Location: ....

Today

The weather was _____

and the temperature was

_____

My favorite food
we tried today was

Today we traveled by

....

Today we went to see

_____

_____

_____

_____

Today

I was most excited to see

_____

_____

_____

_____

_____

_____

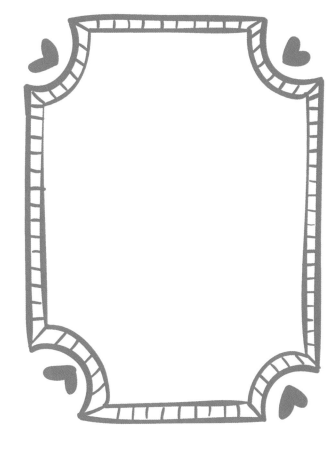

I want to

Remember

_____

_____

_____

_____

_____

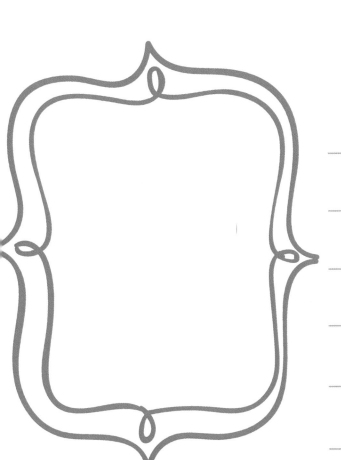

Daily Journal

day #

Location: ....

Today

The weather was

_____

and the temperature was

_____

My favorite food
we tried today was

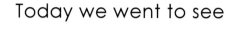
Today we went to see

_____

_____

_____

_____

_____

_____

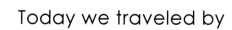
Today we traveled by

....

Today

I was most excited to see

_____

_____

_____

_____

_____

_____

I want to

Remember

_____

_____

_____

_____

_____

Daily Journal

day #

Location: ....

Today

The weather was

_____

and the temperature was

_____

Today we went to see ....

My favorite food we tried today was

_____

_____

_____

_____

_____

Today we traveled by ....

Today

I was most excited to see

_____
_____
_____
_____
_____
_____
_____

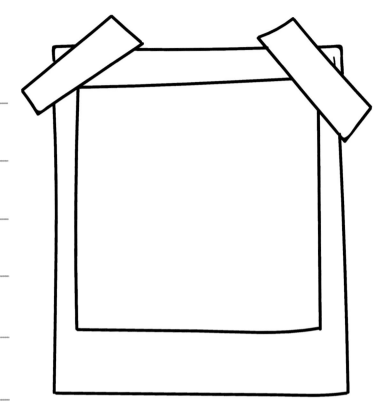

I want to

Remember

_____
_____
_____
_____
_____
_____

Daily Journal

day #

Location: ....

Today

The weather was _____

and the temperature was

My favorite food
we tried today was

_____

Today we traveled by

....

Today we went to see

_____

_____

_____

_____